The Police Are Not Your Friends

Guide to Police Interaction, Detainment, Arrest and Trial

- another guide from -

T Fitz

Monterey Publishing

ISBN: 978-1-7375787-2-7

Dedication

This book, as most anything I do, is dedicated to my son. Zeke, your dad has been in the biggest fight of his life working to protect you. My son, you are the best thing I have ever been a part of. I love you. I will always be here for you, no matter what. Why? Because that's my job.

Disclaimer

I am not a legal professional. Just a guy who's been through his fair share of arrests and court battles, civil and criminal. The advice given here is by no means meant to be comprehensive or even fully accurate. Please consult an attorney for proper advice. You are responsible for the decisions you make. I cannot take on that responsibility for you. That being said, I hope some of the information included in this book goes on to help at least one person sometime down the road. If I have done that, then I will count this a success. Should any of my work ever bring about true and positive change in our society, I will count that as a victory. As Edward Bulwer-Lytton said, "The pen is mightier than the sword."

CONTENTS

Introduction

As a child, I was brought up to believe the police existed to serve and protect my family, as well as our neighbors; all the people of our country. I was taught that anyone who got arrested was a bad person and the police were saving our society from these bad people. Being quite an inquisitive child, one day I asked my dad if he had ever been arrested.

He looked down at me with that loving fatherly smile and told me the truth: "Yes."

I immediately furrowed my brow in confusion. I don't believe I inquired further, but this threw a kink into my belief system. If people who get arrested are bad and my dad had been arrested, yet I knew my dad was a good man, then how could all people who get arrested be bad?

Of course, as children, we perceive a lot of the world and the way things are in much of a black-or-white, good-or-bad, yes-or-no sort of way. The truth is most things exist in an area of gray. The judicial system, including those on the front lines we refer to as law-enforcement officers, certainly exist in this gray area. There are ones who are good, honest, and there to protect you; ones who are unscrupulous and abuse the power they are granted, and ones that fill out the spectrum in the middle. However, know there are some constants that all officers of the law share and specific methods they use which you should be aware of. Knowledge is power, and, as we are taught by G.I. Joe, knowing is half the battle. This knowledge is especially important in regard to tactics used against the accused. Stick with me; we will get there.

The fact is that many of us will get arrested at some point in our lives. The Brennan Center for Justice's reports at *brennancenter.org* that by age twenty-three nearly one in three Americans will have been arrested.[10] Mellissa McFadden tells stories of the falsely accused in her book *Destructive Lies*, all of which involved an arrest. I myself have been locked in the silver bracelets. I have actually been arrested four times in my forty years on Earth. Yep, if you do the math there, that is an average of once per decade of life. I have learned a lot through these arrests and thought it pertinent to share what I have learned with others. We will also go over some police encounters other individuals and families have unfortunately found themselves involved in.

There are many insidious instances under which you could find yourself arrested or detained, but before further discussing police interaction, I thought it would be wise to familiarize you with three of your utmost important safeguards: the rights granted to each citizen of the United States of America under the 4th, 5th, and 6th Amendments to our Constitution. Knowing your rights is critical and will aid you in processing the information put forth in the rest of this book.

Your Constitutional Rights and Why You Should Exercise Them

I'm sure you've heard about the Bill of Rights. Also known as the first 10 Amendments to the United States Constitution, granting civil rights and liberties to the individual. It starts off by granting freedom of speech, press, and religion, then ends stating the Federal Government has only the powers listed, delegating everything else to the individual states. For the purposes of police interaction and potential arrest, we are going to focus on the rights granted under the 4th, 5th, and 6th Amendments. I will tell you that the business cards of many criminal lawyers will give you the exact verbiage to recite if you are being detained, stating that you are exercising these three rights. Knowing these rights is imperative, so let's get to it!

4th Amendment - Search and Seizure

The right of the people to be secure in their persons, houses, papers, and effects, against unreasonable searches and seizures, shall not be violated, and no Warrants shall issue, but upon probable cause, supported by Oath or affirmation, and particularly describing the place to be searched, and the persons or things to be seized.

It starts with security of your person against unreasonable search and seizure. In simple terms, this means the government can't go through your pockets, handbags, backpacks, etc. There are now many laws and statues that can strip you of this right for various reasons, but at its base level, the 4th Amendment grants you the right to deny such a search. This then extends to your home, papers, and effects. Notice, however, the use of the word *unreasonable* and the phrase *probable cause*. Both are gray areas and encompass the ability to bypass your 4th Amendment privileges. The framers of our Constitution only grant us protection against *unreasonable* search and seizure. I shall expound on this shortly.

Also, the 4th Amendment states that no warrant shall be issued against any of us without probable cause supported by someone's oath or affirmation. It further states that, should a warrant be issued, it must be descriptive of the place or places to be searched and what the officers conducting the search are there to try and find. As you can see, this is not an absolute right granting protection against search and seizure.

You may think this only matters if you are a criminal; that if you have nothing to hide, you have nothing to worry about. I assure you, this is not always the case, and you should know your rights. When, where, and how police can conduct a search falls under the general topic of criminal procedure. We noted that your 4th Amendment protections no longer apply if a warrant is issued and that the issuing of a warrant may be granted upon demonstration of probable cause. This means that a warrant should not be issued just on suspicion or an anonymous tip; although, I must say that sometimes judges issue warrants on pretty flimsy probable cause.

Notice when I mentioned warrants, I stated "if" they are issued? This is because despite the fact that it seems the police would always need a warrant, the courts have ruled that a warrant is not always required for the police to engage in a reasonable search. What makes a reasonable search is a question that the courts have long wrestled with. Let me just state that the police can easily claim probable cause. For instance, they can search your car if they claim to smell marijuana. That is even if there is no marijuana in your car and you have never even considered smoking grass of any ilk.

One of the most important Supreme Court cases dealing with searches and seizures is *Mapp v. Ohio*, decided in 1961. This case resulted in what I consider to be a pretty wild outcome. Officers were dispatched to the home of Dollree Mapp to conduct a search for explosives and gambling equipment. They did not have a warrant and were denied consent to enter the premises by Mrs. Mapp. The officers left, only to come back a little later where they would present a fake warrant and search the home. No explosives or gambling equipment were found, but they did uncover a trunk of illegal pornography. Not the kind that would be illegal today, just pornography, which was illegal at the time. This led to the arrest of Mrs. Mapp, with the main evidence against her being the pornography, but the officers' probable cause was to search for explosives. The court ruled that the evidence had been seized through an illegal search. There was no warrant, and even if there had been one, it probably wouldn't have included the trunk in which they found the you-know-what.

More importantly, they ruled that this evidence and any evidence seized pursuant to an illegal search cannot be used against a defendant at trial. This is known as the exclusionary rule.[11]

As you can see, there are some valid protections you have against the police searching your home, but there are also some exceptions, many of which involve your car.

As mentioned, the courts have been fairly lenient when the police feel a need to search your vehicle. This is mostly because when they pull you over, it is likely for a moving violation, like speeding, which can be considered probable cause. Especially if they think you are speeding away from a crime. I will say that the court decisions on this are really complicated, but the general rule of thumb is that the police can generally search your car and person if they pull you over. Regardless (this is not legal advice), you should state, and hopefully record, that you are not consenting to the search.

On the topic of searches, it is important to mention that there are a group of people who don't have the same protections we've discussed. These people are students. The courts have ruled that students don't have the same protections as other citizens and that the interest of the state in keeping a safe, drug/weapon-free education environment trumps a student's right to privacy. There are, however, some limits as to how intrusive these searches can be. Yep, no drop 'em, bend over and cough for the students.

We brought up traffic stops and will go over them in more detail later in this guide, but for now, let's go ahead and move on the rights granted under the 5th Amendment.

5th Amendment - Don't Talk to the Police!

No person shall be held to answer for a capital, or otherwise infamous crime, unless on a presentment or indictment of a grand jury, except in cases arising in the land or naval forces, or in the militia, when in actual service in time of war or public danger; nor shall any person be subject for the same offense to be twice put in jeopardy of life or limb; nor shall be compelled in any criminal case to be a witness against himself, nor be deprived of life, liberty, or property, without due process of law; nor shall private property be taken for public use, without just compensation.

The first question one may have when reading the 5th Amendment is "What is a *capital,* or *otherwise infamous crime*?". Simply put, a capital crime is any crime that is punishable by death. As for an infamous crime, this goes back to a speech James Madison presented to congress, which would become the 5th Amendment, where he used the term "infamous crime". This has later been refined to basically mean a felony or any crime punishable by more than one year of imprisonment.

To prosecute these crimes, the prosecution must first present their evidence relating to said crime before a grand jury. Through this, the prosecution can obtain an indictment. This process may be confusing to some, and justifiably so. I also believe the process varies to some degree depending on what state you live in, but basically, a grand jury is simply a jury to which the prosecution presents evidence of guilt behind closed doors, who then determines if the evidence presented is enough to move forward with prosecuting the alleged charges. This is known as an indictment. There is a saying among criminal attorneys that a grand jury would indict a sandwich. Basically, this means if your case is presented to a grand jury, you can expect an indictment.

The 5th Amendment grants exceptions to the military, who have their own process. It also grants exceptions to the militia. In the early days of our country, well-regulated militias played a very important role, but they seem to have become close to extinct in today's society. That, of course, is an entirely other topic.

The 5th Amendment then goes on to state that a person cannot be tried for the same crime twice. You will often hear this referred to as double jeopardy. If a person is tried for a crime and found innocent but later proven guilty by other means, that person cannot be tried for the same crime again. That sounds wrong on the surface, but it's an important right as the use of double jeopardy could easily be subjected to abuse by our justice system.

Next and most importantly, the 5th Amendment gives you the right to avoid self-incrimination. Yep, that is where you get the right to remain silent upon arrest, detainment, or any sort of police interrogation. This right was further expounded upon in the famous case *Miranda v. Arizona*, where the Supreme Court's decision addressed four different cases, arising from lower-level appellate courts, involving custodial interrogations. Custodial meaning the person accused is in the custody of law enforcement. In each case, the defendant was questioned by authorities in a private room yet not made aware of their rights at the onset of the interrogation process. This case resulted in a person now having to be made aware of their aptly named "Miranda Rights" prior to interrogation. Many confuse this, thinking they must be read these rights upon arrest, but the accused only has to be read their Miranda Rights before any interrogation ensues.

Further, most believe those who invoke their right to remain silent do so to hide their guilt. This isn't always the case; many of these people are just being smart and know how the law works. Look at the case of *Ullman v. United States*, where the Supreme Court stated, "Too many, even those who should be better advised, view this privilege as a shelter for wrongdoers. They too readily assume that those who invoke it are either guilty of [a] crime or commit perjury claiming the privilege." Even if you feel like remaining silent makes you look guilty, it's better to keep your mouth shut. Please read on and allow me to prove this and help guide you on what you should do in case of detainment and police interrogation. We will get there in a later chapter, but first let's come to understand our rights granted under the 6th Amendment.

6th Amendment - Right to Counsel and Due Process

In all criminal prosecutions, the accused shall enjoy the right to a speedy and public trial, by an impartial jury of the state and district wherein the crime shall have been committed, which district shall have been previously ascertained by law, and to be informed of the nature and cause of the accusation; to be confronted with the witnesses against him; to have compulsory process for obtaining witnesses in his favor, and to have the assistance of counsel for his defense.

As read, the 6th Amendment applies to all criminal prosecutions. It grants you the right to a quick, speedy, public trial, and to have that trial decided by an impartial jury. Firstly, I will tell you that the term quick and speedy is used quite loosely. In most cases, that means the prosecution will have two years to set a date for the defendant's trial. There are some cases, for certain felonies, where that timeline is extended by a year. As to the jury, it is important to know that often you must request a jury, otherwise the presiding judge will be making the final decision on your guilt or innocence. I cannot offer legal advice, but if I am to be judged, I will ensure it is by an impartial jury. Jury selection is a process in itself and can take some time. Know that if you are paying a criminal-defense attorney, it is very likely that requesting a jury will cost you more money due to the amount of time involved in juror selection. This is where you have to ask yourself if you can put a price on your freedom.

The 6th Amendment also grants you the right to be informed of the crime for which you are being accused and the nature of said crime. This is the right to know if you are being accused of a misdemeanor or felony and the severity that is attached (felony one, felony two, etc.). You also have the right to face your accuser(s) and any witness against you at trial. That is an important right. It means someone can't just accuse you of a crime and that be that. They must submit to the trial process. As stated, you are also allowed a process that makes the appearance at court of anyone with evidence in your favor (known as exculpatory evidence) compulsory; meaning, they must come forth and present that evidence at trial.

Finally, you have the right to counsel. This differs from your right to counsel during interrogation granted under the 5th Amendment, in that you have the right to counsel during all critical stages of criminal prosecution. The Supreme Court defined the critical stages of prosecution to include arraignment, post indictment line-ups, post-indictment interrogation, plea negotiations, and entering a plea of guilty.

Some of us may not be familiar with some of that terminology. I know I didn't always know the difference between an arraignment and an indictment. An arraignment is where you enter a plea to the court. This will be guilty, not guilty, or no contest (there are actually three other plea options we will briefly go over later in this guide). The latter means you do not admit guilt but will accept the penalties for the charge(s). Indictment, on the other hand, is where you are formally charged. Depending on the severity of the crime, this will come from either the district attorney or be handed down from a grand jury. We will go into more detail on the grand jury process later in this guide.

Know that criminal proceedings begin with a formal charge being issued, a preliminary hearing, indictment, or arraignment. Just being arrested does not necessarily mean the start of criminal proceedings, unless a formal charge has been issued. Without that, you are not privy to the protections granted under the 6th Amendment.

If you cannot afford an attorney, one will be provided for you. This person is referred to as a public, or indigent, defender. I have dealt with public defenders. I can tell you they have more work than they can handle, and even the ones who truly care about the outcome of your case don't have the time to properly prepare your defense. Think about this: what do they call a lawyer who graduated at the bottom of their class? Yeah, they call them a lawyer, and that is probably the one you will have representing you should you not be able to procure the funds to hire an adequate attorney.

Chances are, they are going to try to work out a plea deal where you plead guilty and accept certain terms, even if you are innocent. Again, this is not legal advice, but if you find yourself accused of a crime, I urge you to do whatever it takes to obtain a good criminal attorney who specializes in the sort of crime for which you are accused.

Arrest and Detainment
How it happens and what to do

Now that we have gone over the rights granted under the US Constitution, let's talk about being detained or arrested. As stated in the introduction, many of us will find ourselves in this situation at one point or another. There are multiple ways that an arrest or detainment can commence, but the two main ways that come to mind are through traffic stops or the knock and talk. Let's break down each of these and go over what you should do if you find yourself in either of these situations.

Traffic Stops

Considering the vast majority of people issued a driver's license in the United States will at some point be pulled over, we will start there. We should all be familiar with our rights, as well as our obligations, during a traffic stop. Certain laws and police practices vary from state to state, and it is a good idea to familiarize yourself with those particulars, but for our purposes, we will cover information that pertains to all fifty states.

There are a wide variety of reasons a person could get pulled over: not wearing a seatbelt, speeding, improper lane usage, a burned-out lightbulb, having the appearance of another vehicle that is fleeing from a crime, and a multitude of other reasons. For the minor violations, you can certainly be stopped, and not only for the violation — it can give the officer the chance to perform the old stop, look, and sniff. They will be looking for anything in your vehicle that may be illegal, looking at your demeanor and sniffing for the presence of drugs or alcohol. Any of these could be considered probable cause and escalate a simple traffic stop into something far more serious. Regardless, let's run through a traffic stop and discuss best practices for certain situations.

If an officer is behind you with their lights on, you need to pull over. If you have a recording device, use it. You never know what evidence may help you in the future. If you don't feel safe, or feel the officer is not legitimate, you may continue driving to a safe, well-lit spot. Should this be the case and you cannot pull over immediately, indicate to the officer that you are going to comply and that you will pull over. Slow down and turn on your hazard lights. You may call 911 and remain on the phone with the operator while you stop and verify the officer's identity. Once you do pull over and stop, make sure you keep your hands where the officer can see them. You definitely don't want the officer to get the impression you are going for a weapon, as that could end with devastating results.

You will be asked for your license, registration, and proof of insurance. You should comply with these requests. You may be asked to exit the vehicle. In the United States, you are not breaking the law if an officer asks you to exit and you kindly refuse; remember though, an officer asking and officer ordering are two different scenarios, so let's briefly go over them both.

If the officer says, "Would you mind stepping out of the car, ma'am?" and you say, "No, thank you," that is legal. However, if the officer *orders* you out of the vehicle and you refuse, you can be arrested for refusing to obey an officer's lawful order. The specific crime will depend upon the local statute's verbiage, but it will probably be something like "disobeying a peace officer" or "obstructing a peace officer."[7] This authority comes from the US Supreme Court's ruling in *Pennsylvania v. Mimms*, 434 U.S. 106 (1997), and was later extended to also give them the authority to order passengers out of the vehicle in *Maryland v. Wilson*, 519 U.S. 408 (1997).

Regardless, if asked to exit the vehicle, it may be a good idea to calmly exit, while stating that you are exiting based on the officer's request and not because you consent to a search. Then again, the decision is up to you. Feel free to ask them if their request is an order, and if it isn't, kindly state that you would prefer to remain seated.

To reiterate, during a simple traffic stop, you are required to present identification and proof of insurance;

potentially, registration information as well. Depending on the locality, that may be all that is required of you by law. This is where you need to research and study laws pertaining to the state and locality of where you reside or frequent. Knowing your rights is imperative.

Other than these few things, you have no further obligation to the officer at this point of the traffic stop. As in all the situations we will discuss, the officer performing the stop will ask you some questions. Many think that being fully compliant and doing whatever the officer says or answering any question they ask will give them a better chance at having their ticket thrown out, but this is just a myth.

They will most likely question you regarding the perceived violation and ask other general questions about where you are going. They do this to collect evidence. Again, whether you know it or not, they are most likely performing the old stop, look and sniff. They are looking at you and in your vehicle for signs of inebriation and sniffing you for evidence of alcohol or drugs. Hopefully, you are smart enough to not drive in that condition, but it is known to happen. At this moment, the officer is looking for anything that can be used as probable cause for a search.

Remember, you still have rights. Especially the right to remain silent. While the police may require you to tell them your name (depending on the state), they may not legally require you to tell them about your immigration status, where you're travelling from, where you're going, or what you're doing. Don't let them trick you. It is almost a certainty the officer will ask you questions that you don't have to answer. Answers to these questions, no matter how seemingly innocent, can be twisted and used against you! For example:

Officer: "Where are you coming from?"

You: "I was attending my niece's graduation. We just stopped for gas and snacks at the 7-11 and are heading home."

Maybe an incident just happened at that 7-11. Well, now you're a suspect and a candidate for detainment.

Should you decide to exercise your right to remain silent, and you should, you must communicate that fact. The Supreme Court decided that simply remaining silent is not an effective way to exercise the right. Even if you haven't done anything wrong, remember that lying to the police is a crime, but remaining silent is not!

Although you can't lie to the police, it is important to know that they can lie to you! Never let an officer trick you into thinking they will throw out your ticket if you comply with a request to search your vehicle. You have the right to refuse. Just take your ticket and politely ask if you are free to go. You have the right to ask if you are being detained. If you are not, then you are free to get back on the road.

Sign the ticket if asked. It is simply a confirmation you received the ticket, not an admission of guilt. Refusing this request may needlessly escalate the encounter. Know you can dispute the charges later in court.

Hopefully, the traffic stop won't go any further than previously discussed, but it very well could. If it does, then by now, you should have already asked if you are being detained and told that you are indeed. If this is the case, the officer likely wants to search your vehicle in the hopes of finding illicit drugs. In many states, an officer with no probable cause can order a dog to walk around your car to see if they *alert* the officer, justifying a full search. One issue with police dogs is that they want to please their handlers. They know the handler wants them to provide an *alert*, and this has caused many to be improperly detained. The laws have a long way to go in this area.

Believe it or not, in many areas, the police don't even need reasonable suspicion, which lacks the concrete evidence to be probable cause, to use drug dogs to sniff a vehicle during a legitimate traffic stop. This stems from a case that made it to the Supreme Court, *Illinois v. Caballes*.

Roy Caballes was pulled over for speeding and subsequently arrested for marijuana trafficking after a drug dog was brought out and signaled something in his vehicle. Caballes appealed his conviction on the grounds of a violation of his 4th Amendment rights. Justice Stevens wrote the opinion of the court, finding that since dog sniffs only identify the presence of illegal items, in which case citizens have no legitimate privacy interest, the 4th Amendment does not apply to the use of dogs. This ruling gives police the right to walk a drug dog around your vehicle during any legitimate traffic stop. If the dog signals, then officers have probable cause to conduct a search.

Notice the use of the word legitimate? It's important to understand the implication of that word in this context. The legitimacy of a traffic stop depends on its duration. The police do not have the right to detain you indefinitely until a dog arrives. Basically, if the police can't bring a dog to the scene in the time it takes to run your tags and write a ticket, the use of the dog becomes constitutionally suspect. Usually, the officer won't have a dog on hand,

and although they don't need reasonable suspicion to use one, they do need reasonable suspicion to detain you. If you are being detained, remember you have the right to determine if you can leave by asking, "Officer, am I free to go?" If the officer refuses and detains you until the dog comes, you still have the right to remain silent and refuse consent to any searches.

You also have the right to refuse to consent to the dog sniff, even if the officer tells you that you must. You must be aware that unlocking your car at the officer's request or handing them your keys is the same as consenting to a search. You always have the right to refuse by stating, "Officer, I don't consent to any searches." (Repeat, if necessary.) If a judge determines that the officer had no justification for detaining you until the dog arrived, any evidence discovered by the dog may be thrown out in court.

It's very important to know the laws around traffic stops for your state and any states you may end up visiting while driving. A few quick google searches should get you mostly up to speed. There is also a plethora of YouTube videos out there created by First Amendment auditors and their ilk, providing you valuable information on the subject. One that comes to mind is *Audit the Audit*. I suggest checking out their channel as a start on your journey to informing yourself of your rights. I can't place enough stress on the point that knowing your rights is a must.

Maybe you believe knowing your rights in this area isn't as important as stated. You never carry anything illegal in your car, you abide by traffic laws, and you have nothing to hide. I hate to bring race into this, but maybe you think this because you are white. There are many stories where someone of color was badly injured or killed during a normal traffic stop. That is a whole other subject, but regardless of race, if you hold the belief that you have nothing to worry about, you are making an assumption based on the premise that the police are your friends.

The unfortunate reality is that not all officers of the law have integrity. I am not saying that applies to all officers, but you always have the chance of being stopped by one of the bad seeds. In that scenario, you never know what sort of charge(s) you could face or what sort of evidence could be planted to make an arrest. Feel free to check out a study done in April of 2016: *Police Integrity Lost: A Study of Law Enforcement Officers Arrested.*[6]

I hate to sound like a broken record, but I feel it's important. Know your rights!

Knock and Talk

Next is the knock and talk. Any officer who has ever been dispatched to a residence knows the workings of the good old knock and talk. This is a common tactic used by every policing agency. It basically goes like this: the authorities have obtained some evidence via one of their channels of information gathering. To be clear, law-enforcement agencies get information every day; it could be from a call to one of their 800-number tip lines, a 911 or non-emergency call from someone in the neighborhood, through one of their informants, or even through social media. Trust me, those methods just scratch the surface in regard to all the methods law enforcement uses to gain information. Believe me, law enforcement has a plethora of systems as a means to this end. Their informers have informers! Regardless, for our purposes, let's say a neighbor has something against you and lacks the integrity and candor of handling whatever it is like an adult. They call the police and provide information. The information communicated could relate to a disturbance, testimony of illicit drug activity, or any illicit activity for that matter, and officers have been dispatched to investigate.

Information acquired in this manner is known as heresy. It does not meet the standards of probable cause and is not grounds to obtain a warrant to search the premises. Without either of those, law-enforcement officers cannot enter your home. As with most things legal, there are a few exceptions we shall discuss further, but in the majority of knock and talk situations, the police do not have any reason to enter your home. They cannot even enter what is known as the curtilage of your home, the area of enclosed land around your home. Your fenced in backyard is an example of curtilage.

As to the knock and talk, an officer or officers will come to your door and knock, hoping to engage you in conversation in an attempt to gain additional information. I hope you are already recording the incident by now, as this is how it goes: they will say, "Hi, I'm Officer Smith. This is Officer Jones. We've got information that (insert x, y, z, here). Some examples would be, "We've got information that you are growing marijuana inside your home," "We've got information that you were at a location where a crime was committed," or anything you could imagine that could come down to illegal activity. Then, they will ask if you will allow them to come inside. Maybe they say they just want to talk, asking to come in, preying on our innate desire to be polite to others.

What they are doing here is attempting to get inside your residence via your consent. Remember, they don't have a basis to come inside without your consent. If they had anything that wouldn't require your consent, they wouldn't be knocking. Your door would be opened for you by any means possible.

If you do give consent, anything they view, find, or seize while inside your home can be used as evidence to prosecute you in court. Remember, they are there to gain evidence. Maybe you have nothing to hide, and I hope that is the case, but even so, it is advised you not talk to the police.

Leave your door locked and do not respond. Contact an attorney and have them handle the situation. Yes, it will cost some money, but knowing words can be misconstrued and used against you in the future, an attorney is always the best route to take. I am aware that most of us can't afford to drop the money on an attorney. If that is the case, it is still in your best interest not to talk to the police. Should they want to pursue the claims, and you eventually find yourself detained and interrogated, an attorney will be provided for you. I hate to say it, but most public defenders are not going to put in the legwork that a criminal case requires. They do, however, know the law and are highly familiar with these situations. In the best-case scenario of a knock and talk, the police leave, and you never hear from them again. That can happen.

Before we end this section, I think it is important that you know we will be further hammering home the fact that talking to the police cannot help you; it can only hurt you. We will go over specific cases in the section on detainment. Stick with me.

Warrantless Entry

After having discussed tactics police deploy to gain your consent to enter your home, it may be pertinent to briefly go over circumstances when the police could enter your home without you having provided a form of consent. We all know that should the police arrive with a warrant, they will enter your home by any means necessary. You may not even know they have a warrant because you locked your doors and didn't answer, but if this is the case, you will know soon enough and potentially be left with a broken doorframe. Of course, if you are in that situation, a broken doorframe is the least of your worries. Regardless, warrants, probable cause (including officer(s) seeing something illegal in plain sight), and consent aren't the only avenues police have to gain legal entry to your residence. This is where the exception of exigent (meaning, something is pressing or demanding) circumstances comes into play.

The main case that will come up in regard to this exception is *Kentucky v King*, 563 U.S. 452 (2011), where the Supreme Court held that warrantless searches conducted in police-created exigent circumstances do not violate the Fourth Amendment as long as the police do not create the exigency by violating or threatening to violate the Fourth Amendment. The Court decided a search or seizure without a warrant is presumptively unreasonable; however, exigent circumstances are an exception to this presumption. They further identified three exigent circumstances: emergency aid, hot pursuit, and destruction of evidence.

It started in Lexington, Kentucky, where police officers set up a drug-buy outside an apartment complex, using an undercover informant being surveilled by an undercover officer. After the suspect sold crack-cocaine to the informant, uniformed officers were called in to pursue the suspect. They lost sight of the suspect in a breezeway but had just heard a door close. At the end of the breezeway, they found two doors, one on the left and the other on the right, and were not sure which the suspect may have used. They did, however, claim to smell burning marijuana coming from the apartment on the left. According to testimony, the officers banged on the door, announcing, "This is the police," and then heard movements leading them to believe evidence was being destroyed.

After kicking in the door, they found Hollis King, his girlfriend, and a guest who was smoking marijuana. Upon a further search of the apartment, they found cash, drugs, and paraphernalia. King was charged and entered a conditional plea of guilty in the Fayette Circuit Court, where he reserved his right to appeal the denial of his motion entered to suppress evidence obtained from what was argued to be an illegal search and seizure. King was sentenced to eleven years in prison, and the Kentucky

Court of Appeals affirmed the conviction, holding that exigent circumstances supporting the warrantless search were not of the police's making and that police did not engage in deliberate and intentional conduct to evade the warrant requirement.

Later in 2010, the Kentucky Supreme Court reversed the court order, finding the officer's entry to the residence to have broken Mr. King's rights provided under the Fourth Amendment, deciding what the officers had heard was not sufficient to provide them exigent circumstances. Their reasoning was that police can't rely on exigent circumstances that are reasonably foreseeable from their own officers' actions.

This decision eventually made its way up to the US Supreme Court, where Justice Samuel Alito delivered the Court's majority opinion, holding that assuming for the purpose of argument, exigent circumstances existed, the rule applied in this case because the officers did not create the exigency by violating or threatening to violate the Fourth Amendment. Yep, our Fourth Amendment rights took one on the chin that day.

Justice Alito further clarified the police-created exigency doctrine, which had been percolating in the lower courts, by explaining that to answer that question, just as with any other Fourth Amendment question, is reasonableness: "The exigent-circumstances rule justifies a warrantless search when the conduct of the police preceding the exigency is reasonable in the same sense." The decision here was that warrantless entry was reasonable in order to prevent possible destruction of evidence. The decision of the lower court was reversed, and the lower court was further remanded.

This decision, however, was not unanimous. Justice Ruth Bader Ginsburg, in her dissenting opinion, contended that the majority opinion of the court did in fact allow police to dishonor our protections provided under the Fourth Amendment's warrant requirement in drug cases. Unfortunately, majority rules in this case. Luckily for Mr. King, later in 2012, the Kentucky Supreme Court did reverse the previous decision regarding the motion to suppress evidence, deciding that the prosecution had not met its burden of proof in proving exigent circumstances to justify a warrantless entry, as the sounds inside the apartment were indistinguishable from ordinary household sounds, and his conviction was overturned.[8]

To provide an example of exigent circumstances where a warrantless entry may be upheld, consider a 911 call being made from a residence, or thought to be made from a residence, where the caller says a child is in danger, and the police arrive at the wrong residence. In a case like this, officers will most likely enter the property without a warrant, claiming exigent circumstances.

Maybe the police hear screams or cries for help coming from inside a residence. This, too, could warrant exigent circumstances.

Hopefully this has helped you to gain insight into situations when law enforcement may enter your residence without a warrant. For a brief review, the warrant requirement does not need to be met when any of these situations can be shown: search incident to arrest (as would have been in the previous case if the officers had entered the correct apartment), consent search, something illegal being in plain view, automobile exception, border-search exception (which we have not covered; regarding international borders), and exigent circumstances.

Detainment

Let's be blunt. Police make a living by arresting people, and they have a bag of tricks to make it happen. Deception is a part of law-enforcement training and tactics. There are a lot of myths floating around out there about police tactics; what is legal and what isn't. A lot of people don't even know the police can lie to them! Many people wrapped up in the world of illegal activities believe if they ask an undercover officer if they are a cop, then that officer must tell them the truth, but that's not the case. It's through these deceptive tactics deployed by law enforcement during traffic stops, knock and talks, and any other sort of police interaction that you could find yourself being detained. I hope you never find yourself in that situation, but if you do, it's important you know the ins and outs in order to handle the circumstance.

If you are detained or arrested, it's very important you let the arresting officer know you are invoking your 5th Amendment right to remain silent and that you keep your mouth shut. This goes even if you are innocent. Everything you say is evidence that can be used against you. Look at what Justice Robert Jackson of the Supreme Court had to say: "[A]ny lawyer worth his salt will tell the suspect in no uncertain terms to make no statement to the police under any circumstances." Please remember that. You'd be amazed how many people, well-educated on law, haven't taken this advice and subsequently got convicted based upon their own words.

Even criminal-defense attorneys. A story can be found in the *Virginia Pilot* about an experienced criminal-defense lawyer who ended up being convicted of criminal assault because he talked to the police. He was accused of assaulting another attorney in the hallway. There were no other witnesses to this. A woman said he grabbed her by the throat during an argument over the case, and he denied it. At trial it should have been his word against hers. He stated that he didn't even touch her. Unfortunately for him, when police had approached him earlier and asked if he would be willing to answer some questions, he complied, thinking, *Sure, why not? I'm an experienced criminal-defense attorney. I'm savvy and accustomed to dealing with the police*, and he provided them with a statement. The statement he gave was not recorded. When the case went to trial, it was no longer his word against hers, as the officer he'd spoken with took the stand and testified that when he'd questioned the defendant, he'd said he did indeed put his hand on her throat but just as a joke. Then the defendant had to take the stand again and state that he never said that during questioning, that the officer was incorrect in his statement. Now it was his word against the word two people. Who was telling the truth? We'll never know for sure, but what we do know is that he was found guilty.[1]

The heat of the problem, as Justice Breyer of the US Supreme Court explained in 1998, is "the complexity of modern federal criminal law, codified in several thousand sections of the United States Code and the virtually infinite variety of factual circumstances that might trigger an investigation into a possible violation of the law, make it difficult for anyone to know, in advance, just when a particular set of statements might later appear (to a prosecutor) to be relevant to some such investigation." Believe it or not, even the federal government has lost count of the actual number of federal crimes, as they are scattered all over the US Code, encompassing roughly 27,000 pages.

One you may have never heard about is called the Lacey Act, which makes it a federal offense for any person to import, export, transport, sell, receive, acquire, or purchase any fish, wildlife, or plant taken, possessed, transported, or sold in violation of any law, treaty, or regulation of the United States or in violation of any Indian tribal law or any law or regulation of any State or any foreign law. Yeah. And people have been convicted of this because they brought back a Boney Fish from Honduras, not knowing that Honduran law, not American — Honduran — forbade the possession of the Boney Fish. The point being that there are a ton of laws, and it's impossible to truly know if you are breaking any of them at any given moment. There's over 10,000 ways you may implicate yourself! A great reason to keep your mouth shut when talking to the police![1]

If I haven't convinced you by now that talking to the police is a bad idea, let's go over seven reasons to solidify for ourselves that talking to the police is never a good idea.

The first reason is that there is no way it can help. You can't talk your way out of getting arrested. Ask any officer that had some evidence of someone's guilt if that person ever once talked themselves out of an arrest. I assure you they haven't! You may not know this, but you can't give the police any information that will help you at trial. Don't believe me? See *Federal Rule of Evidence* 801(d)(2)(A). Everything you tell the police can and will be used against you, but it cannot be used for you. Remember that.

The next reason is that if you are guilty or innocent, you can admit your guilt, yet you get no benefit in return. The guilty should be punished and should have to pay for their crimes. I believe we can all agree to that, but what's the rush? If you look at statistics from federal court, you will find that around 86% of defendants plead guilty at some point before trial. The large majority of cases will not make it to trial. Perhaps you can work out some sort of arrangement before trial and avoid a harsher sentence while still paying your debt to society. Just a thought.

Have you heard of the Innocence Project, which uses DNA evidence to exonerate the innocent we hold in our prisons? In more than 25% of these cases, the innocent defendant made incriminating statements, delivered outright confessions, or pled guilty. Mind blowing. Don't believe me? Look at Eddie Joe Lloyd who served seventeen years in a Michigan prison for a rape and murder he didn't commit. He was convicted in 1984 of brutally raping and subsequently murdering a 16-year-old girl after writing police with suggestions on how to solve various murders during his stay in a hospital while receiving treatment for mental illness.

Officers visited and interrogated him many times in the hospital, leading him to believe that by confessing and being arrested for these crimes, he would help them track down the real perpetrator. They actually fed him details of the crimes he could not have known, such as the location of the body, type of jeans, and description of earrings the victim was wearing, along with other details of the crime scene. Mr. Lloyd then signed a confession and gave a recorded statement. At trial the prosecution played his confession to the jury and claimed Lloyd had killed the victim in order to get away with the rape. Lloyd was represented pre-trial by a court-appointed attorney who received $150 for pre-trial preparation and investigation. The attorney gave $50 of this money to a convicted felon, who conducted no investigation into Lloyd's mental state or his confession.

Mr. Lloyd's lawyer withdrew from the case eight days before trial was set to commence, and another attorney was appointed, however the trial was not postponed. The trial attorney did not even meet with the pre-trial attorney, nor have time to formulate a proper defense. He called no witnesses and gave a five-minute closing statement. Needless to say, the prosecution got a conviction. It wasn't until the Innocence Project tested semen collected from the victim, exonerating Mr. Lloyd, that he was freed from prison.[2]

I'm sure if you asked the police officers who interrogated Mr. Lloyd why they lied to Mr. Lloyd in gaining a confession, they would tell you that they were just doing their job. More proof that the police are not your friends!

Our third reason to not talk to the police is that even if you are innocent and deny your guilt, it is easy under a stressful situation to get a little carried away and tell some small mistruth or misconstrue a fact that will end up coming back to bite you, and hard. Say you're believed to have committed a murder, armed robbery, or some other heinous crime, and you talk to the police. Imagine how much stress you'd be under; maybe talking fast, stating that you've never killed anyone, never had a gun, was nowhere near that place, etc. Well, if in the heat of the moment, one of the things you said could be proven false, you may end up convicted of a crime you did not commit.

Yet another reason is that even if you are innocent and tell only the truth, you will always, and I emphasize *always*, give the police some information that could help the prosecution gain your conviction. You have to remember that whatever you say could potentially be heard by a jury at trial, and that words are easily twisted and misconstrued. See *Ohio v. Reiner*, where the court states, "We recognized that truthful responses of an innocent witness, as well as those of a wrongdoer, may provide the government with incriminating evidence from the speaker's own mouth." There is no reason to give the police any evidence, because in today's world, as the title of this book states, the police are not your friends.

The fifth reason is that even if you are innocent and speak to the police, telling the truth and only the truth, making no incriminating statements, there is still a chance your answers to their questions can be used to condemn you if the questioning officer doesn't recall your testimony with 100% accuracy. The problem with this is that our memories can become warped over time. This is the way the human mind works: we hear things; we fill in details. This certainly goes for officers that conduct numerous investigations and interrogations. Do you think they can recall all of them with 100% accuracy? I would say that is nearly impossible.

The sixth reason is very similar to the previous one but reversed. Say you talk to the police and tell nothing but the truth and don't say anything incriminating and your answers are even videotaped. The police can't forget your answers in this case, so that negates the previous reason. Well, guess what? Your answers can still be used to condemn you if the officer doesn't recall their questions with 100% accuracy. Isn't that something? You may be wondering how that can happen. Let's assume the police are investigating a shooting and possible murder, and you go to them, stating, "I don't know who killed Bennett. It wasn't me. I have never touched or fired a gun in my life." How could that possibly be used against you? Inconceivable right? Nope; quite simple. All the officer has to do is read that statement to the jury, then the prosecutor asks, "Officer, was there anything about that statement that confused you or surprised you?" The officer replies, "Yes, there was." The prosecutor then asks the officer what about that statement confused or surprised him. The officer then looks at the jury and states, "I never said anything about a shooting. I said we were investigating a murder. He was the one who brought up a gun." You know that wasn't true and take the stand stating it wasn't true. Well, now it's your word against an officer of the law. Funny how that works. Just an innocent mis-recollection by an officer can convict you at trial, even if you're innocent. Please don't forget that fact.

Yet another reason to not talk to the police is that even if you are innocent and tell only the truth, stating nothing incriminating, and the entire interview is videotaped (questions and answers), your answers can still be used against you to gain a conviction. This is even if the police, through no fault of theirs, end up in the possession of any evidence, even mistaken or unreliable evidence, which conveys anything you told them was false. Crazy right? Say you stated you were nowhere near the crime scene, and you weren't, yet the police have interviewed someone you know, someone who has nothing against you, and they swear they saw you near the crime scene around the time of the incident. That person's testimony alone won't convict you (your attorney could have the case thrown out before trial) but, if like a fool, you decided to talk to the police and gave them truthful information on your whereabouts, and now they have a witness — a false, mistaken, confused, but sincere and credible witness — who can testify you were in the vicinity of the crime scene, the prosecutor is likely to get a conviction. They will have the officer take the stand to state you gave a false account of your whereabouts and follow that up with their star witness whose testimony places you where you were not, stating you must have lied when talking to the police. Again, we are back to your word against the state's evidence, and you are likely doomed.[1]

I hope by now, I have shown you that Justice Jackson was correct. Exercise your rights under the 5th Amendment and don't talk to the police. You may just thank me one day.

The Trial Process

Starting with Arrest

If you ever find yourself under arrest after any police interaction, you will find you've become wrapped up in the trial process. It is for this reason that we exercise the rights granted us under the Constitution of the United States, as exercising those rights will be of benefit at this crucial moment in your life.

If you've been arrested and taken to jail, I want you to know what to expect. It isn't fun, but it's not the worst thing that can happen either. If this is your first rodeo, you will probably be a little on edge, but trust me, it's important to stay calm and composed. On top of keeping your mouth shut, and this includes anyone also detained, with whom you may be sharing a cell, I suggest showing respect to the officers.

There was a time I was arrested for public intoxication. It's an embarrassing story, but I'm going to share it to prove the point that kindness can be to your benefit. I was involved in a police interaction and ordered to get back into our vehicle. That man wasn't going to tell *me* what to do. This is America, and I'll stand where I damn well please; the thoughts of a twenty-seven-year-old me.

Well, not cooperating landed me in the silver bracelets and in the backseat of a police cruiser.

It was around midnight on a Friday, and when I was arrested, I was a complete ass; kicking the officer's seat, spewing the nastiest of insults at him for the entire ride to our county jail. I was placed into a drunk tank where I continued to beat the walls and shout profanities. Finally, after I had calmed down, I was put in a small holding cell, with one open toilet and about fifteen to twenty other individuals. This was in Texas, and one thing to know if you are arrested in Texas, and probably many other states, is that you won't be able to have a bond set without first appearing before the magistrate.

I had to stay in that holding cell overnight, as the magistrate wouldn't arrive until morning. Morning rolled around, and I watched as the others I was being held with were taken out to go before the magistrate and be released, whether on their own cognizance or bond. Even people who had been brought in after my arrival. The time was approaching when I knew the magistrate was going to leave, and if that happened, I was the lucky recipient of at least another night in that tank. Finally, I kindly asked an officer if I would be able to get out. He was a little surprised I hadn't been seen yet and thankfully got me that oh-so-lucky last chance in front of the magistrate for the day. Had that not happened, I believe I would have been stuck until Monday morning at the earliest. Instead, I was released without having to post bail.

Why was I held so long? I can only guess, but I am fairly certain it was because of how I'd acted to the arresting officer and then to the officers on the night shift. Oh yeah, they take note of that and have their ways of payback. Believe me on that. It is for that reason I suggest treating the arresting officers and any officers at the jail with the utmost respect.

Regardless, if you find yourself in those silver bracelets and on your way to jail, it's time to face reality. The upcoming hours aren't going to be that great, but in most cases, you will be released between a few to 30ish hours. You may as well accept it.

The last time I was arrested, based on false accusations I might add, I was held for thirty hours in solitary confinement. Believe me, that was no fun. This time I did take the advice given in this book, exercised my rights, and was polite to the deputies of Marion County's Sheriff's Office. Guess what, they were nice to me as well. I ate good meals, the officers would keep in touch with me on when I may be released, and even offered me a book. I ended up reading *I Have Lived A Thousand Years: Growing Up In The Holocaust*. It was about a Jewish woman. She was a survivor of the Holocaust who had even been through the horrors of Auschwitz. Talk about gaining perspective. You find it hard to feel true suffering from a little thirty hours of solitary confinement after reading about what those people went through.

Getting Out of Jail - The Bonds Process

Don't fret too much. You have someone out there who will work to get you released as soon as possible. This person is your interim best friend: the bondsman. In fact, I suggest finding a good bonds agency and keeping their card on your person at all times, just as you do with your identification. Keep reading, and I'll explain why.

Firstly, to expound upon my arrest for public intoxication and getting released from jail, let's dive a little deeper into the process. While you are in a holding cell or on the way to one, the information of your arrest will be presented to a judge or magistrate. That is, unless you are arrested in a place where you must appear before one. Regardless, they will look at the severity of the crime for which you have been accused, as well as other factors regarding your likelihood of appearing at your set court dates, and determine a bond amount. This again will vary between localities. There are also cases where you will be held without bond. If this is the case, then you will not be released until your trial process is complete. Assuming you aren't found guilty, of course.

There are a couple of types of bonds that can be set. Most likely, you will receive a surety bond. This is where you can use a bail-bond agency who will take on the responsibility of your full bond amount should you not appear for your scheduled court appearances. Then there is the cash-only bond. Pray your bond isn't set as cash only, as if that is the case, you better hope you are wealthy. Having a cash-only bond means you can't get a bail-bond agency; you will need to pay the full amount in cash to be released.

For the normal surety bond, you have a couple of options: you can pay the bond amount in full, or call up your new best buddy, the bondsman. Hopefully you can afford one of these options, because if you can't, you will be in the shoes of a person to whom bond was denied and normally arraigned within seventy-two hours. We will discuss the process of arraignment in a later section. Often, if you pay in full and make all of your court appearances, then you will be reimbursed for the bond. This is not always the case, so be sure to check with your attorney should you choose this route.

In most cases, the person arrested, if a bond is set, will choose to bond out using the services of a bondsman (or bondswoman, as the case may be). I must reiterate that having a good bondsman is imperative, as they can often speed up the process of your release. This is why I urge everyone, whether they believe they will ever be arrested or not, to carry the card of a good bondsman with them at all times.

Post Arrest - Arraignment

Now that we have gone over police interactions, detainments, arrests and that oh-so-memorable trip to jail, as well as what to do in those situations, it's time we discuss why knowing and exercising our rights is important. The *why* is actually the most important and critical part, as it will certainly affect your trial and the critical dates along the way.

If you have been charged with a crime and later indicted for that crime, then an arraignment is in your future. It's typically the first court proceeding in a criminal case where you will be advised of your charges and given the opportunity to enter a plea. You can plead guilty, meaning you admit to the charges and are throwing yourself on the mercy of the court; not guilty, stating that you did not commit the crimes for which you are accused; or no contest, meaning that you accept the charges, will take whatever punishment that entails, but do not admit guilt.

Well, those are the most common pleas at an arraignment. There is also the possibility of former judgment of conviction or acquittal, meaning there is already a judgement regarding the charges; double jeopardy, meaning you have already been tried for the same charges; and not guilty by reason of insanity. At your arraignment, one of these six pleas must be made, unless the judge grants a continuance that puts the arraignment off for a reasonable amount of time.

I have personally been involved in four arraignments. The first happened when I was twenty years old. I didn't know my rights and absolutely didn't have the money to ensure my rights were not violated. My rights were clearly violated in this case. There was police misconduct, and it was a huge awakening. It was during this time period a little over twenty years ago thatI lost faith in our legal system, learning the tough fact that you may have rights on paper, but that doesn't matter unless you have a lot of money to back them up.

My second arraignment came a few years later when I was twenty-four. A young gung-ho deputy went for, and obtained, the local record for the most DUI arrests in a single night. I was one of those arrests. I was innocent, but still exercised my rights and refused to submit a breathalyzer. You may be wondering how I ended up in the situation of having red and blue lights flashing behind my vehicle this particular night, and that is a reasonable question. I was driving in the innermost lane meant for traffic in my direction of travel. Yep, that was it. Not speeding, no lights out, registration was valid — just not in the rightmost lane. So I was pulled over for improper lane usage. I was sober. My passenger was far from it. Long story short, I did have a defense attorney, and Hurricane Katrina happened. The state trooper that pulled me over that night was subsequently dispatched to New Orleans for an extended amount of time, missing three consecutive court dates. By having the right to confront my accuser, but my accuser not being available, the court was forced to find me not guilty of the crime. I got a stern talking to from the judge and walked away free of charges. I honestly don't want to think of the consequences exercising my rights may have brought about had the officer been able to make those court appearances.

My third arraignment was the one we previously discussed regarding public intoxication. This is when I learned what a plea of no contest (or *nolo contendere* for the fans of legal Latin) entailed. If this is your plea, you do not admit guilt; the district attorney decides to accept a plea of no contest. This was my offer, and I complied. I paid a fee of around $250, and that was that; over with and behind me. I honestly don't get the no contest plea. How can it be right for a person to pay the price for a crime, yet not admit any guilt in that crime? Guess it's time for a quick history lesson.

Our justice system in America is based on English common law. This goes way back (yeah, I'm getting medieval on you, as that's where this plea has its origins). Who knows the benefits this plea offered a person in medieval times? They could accept punishment but not admit guilt during a time period when even small crimes carried quite harsh punishment. Not only that, but the separation of those in power from the common individual was tremendous. I imagine whole books are written comparing the separation of power and wealth of medieval times to that of today. We certainly don't have time for that, but I can imagine it would be a lot easier for someone in those times to plead *nolo contendere* than to have to fight those in power and later accept the consequences that ensued.[8]

Moving on, my fourth and most current arraignment happened without my presence. It was for the charges I am still fighting to this day, thanks to false accusations. Covid happened, and our courts pretty much shut down with the exception of very pressing cases. Our Sixth Amendment rights took a back seat and were stretched to their limits. I wanted to file a motion for speedy trial and could have, but counsel informed me they could not represent me in the matter if I chose that route. It took the state over six months to gather a grand jury and issue a formal indictment. After that, it was time for arraignment. I had to submit a plea to the charges I had been indicted for. My understanding is that my attorney entered the plea of not guilty on my behalf.

That's it, though. Arraignment is pretty simple: you enter a plea. How long it takes for you to get to this point depends on a few factors. Quite often, the arraignment will be the initial hearing where bond is set. Then again, it could come later if the charges you have are more serious, requiring a grand jury for indictment. If that is the case, and you can't post bond, you will typically be arraigned within seventy-two hours. This timeframe could be extended if bond was posted. Just know that an indictment and an arraignment are two different beasts. The indictment or a filing of formal charges, depending on the situation, happens first. This is followed by the arraignment, where you will enter one of the pleas previously mentioned.

Post Arrest - Discovery

Now comes the discovery phase of the trial process. This is where the state must finally present you with any evidence they have against you. Notice, I said *against* you? Yeah, they can have what is known as exculpatory evidence (evidence showing you did not commit the crime), but they can keep that a secret. At least that is the case in some states and not mandated at the federal level. You will have to check the laws and statutes regarding the state in which you reside to see if exculpatory evidence must be handed over to the defense during the discovery phase.

This is also where witness depositions will be taken. Your attorney will have the opportunity to interview those the prosecution will call to the stand to testify. Being deposed can be intimidating, but the ability to depose witnesses is vital to the discovery process.

Not only are you entitled to any evidence the state has against you, but you must also hand over any evidence you plan to present in your defense. Both sides must have access to all evidence that could be used at trial. This is to level the playing field. There are of course exceptions, but these exceptions are out of the scope of this guide. Just know that the process to this point is arrest, potential for bond, indictment, arraignment, then discovery. Actually, only a small percentage of formal charges will make it this far, and an even smaller percentage will actually go to trial. There are many chances for your plea to be changed and deals to be made along the way. Very few cases, maybe 5%, will actually go to trial, as the stakes can get very high. Many opt out and take a deal before putting their freedom on the line. Maybe I'm hard headed, but should my current charges go to trial, that will be twice in my life that I have taken a case that far. Well, thrice, if you count my second divorce, mercy be!

To expound on evidence, I think we should bring up the recent uptick in the number of officers that wear body cams and the Freedom of Information Act. I suggest you always have your own recording device with you, but even then, you have the right to request any body-cam footage that was recorded during an incident. You have this right through the Freedom of Information Act. The problem is that police can turn their camera off at any time and can potentially "lose" some of the footage. Yeah, like, "I don't know, it seems it just got deleted."

Trust me on this. I was watching a video of body-cam footage, video and audio, gained through the Freedom of Information Act, where an officer tried to detain a man in Colorado for potential trespassing. The man was simply outside picking up trash at his residence and refused the officer's requests. This man stood up for himself and for his rights, while the officer claimed the garbage-collection device was a weapon and further escalated the situation by drawing his weapon. Around eight officers eventually arrived, including the supervisor. It was found the man was doing nothing wrong, and the officers eventually left the scene. Interestingly, when the officer realized he'd messed up, his camera would all of a sudden go black and when he was being told by his supervisor, I am guessing, that he might have overstepped the law, he turned off his audio.[13]

This is why I suggest you maintain your own record. Body-cam footage is often not fully complete, with parts redacted and/or edited. No, it's not right, but that's the reality, so make sure you are prepared at all times. You'll want all the information you can get should you ever be falsely accused of a crime. It happens way more than you might imagine.

Post Arrest - Trial

An in-depth discussion of the entire trial process is outside the scope of this guide, but I thought we would do a brief overview. If you have made it this far in the process, you are in a miniscule percentage of the population. Not only that, but the number of cases that go to trial is on the decline. In 1998, around 7% of cases actually made it to trial. Today, that number is closer to 2%.[12] Why is this? Of course, a lot of factors are involved, but many of the accused, even those that are truly innocent, choose to take a plea. The most likely reason for this is what's known as the "trial penalty." This means that if you choose to go to trial, and lose, you will receive a harsher sentence for exercising your right to trial. How this is the norm and accepted is beyond me. You are incentivized to waive your rights! Land of the free, right? Regardless, you should know that with trial, chance is not in your favor. Most trials are won by the prosecution. It hurts me to say it, but I promise you the scales of justice are tipped.

Moving on, your trial will begin with jury selection. Both sides will have a certain number of jurors they can object to and have removed from the selection process. Also, certain questions will be asked of each juror, and if they seem to have a bias one way or the other, they will most likely be sent home, relieved of their duty. Jury selection can be a long process and is certainly draining on both sides. It does get quite involved. If you are further interested in this process, there is plenty of information out there.

When the day of the trial finally arrives, it will start with opening statements from the prosecution and the defense, followed by witness testimony and cross-examination. Then both sides will provide their closing arguments, the jury will receive their instructions and be sent to deliberate. This is where they will decide upon a verdict. Their decision must be unanimous, or a mistrial will be declared, and the case can be retried. I have even heard of cases where the jury was hung, meaning they could not agree, and the judge told them they must come up with a verdict. That is not true, and that case is in the appeals process as I write. Should the jury agree on a verdict, their verdict will be read aloud in court. Should that verdict be guilty, the defendant will move to the sentencing process where their punishment will be decided.

Speaking of mistrials, there are times when the prosecutor may realize they have messed up and want another chance. There have been times when prosecutors intentionally perform actions they know could result in a mistrial. This decision is that of the judge. Should the judge declare a mistrial, they can do so with or without prejudice. Should they declare a mistrial with prejudice, the prosecution may not have the case tried again. The

opposite is true if a mistrial is granted without prejudice. In that case, the prosecution gets another go at securing their conviction.
After the trial is complete, the appeals process can begin. That too is a whole other beast, but there are a few things to note. An appeal is not like a new trial. Only evidence presented at trial can be used in an appeal. If you wish to appeal evidence, an objection must have been entered during trial. In appeal, they will look for any misuse of the law during the trial process, not retrying the case.

In Conclusion

Hopefully by now, you have a better understanding of police interactions along with the events that lead up to trial and a conviction. I pray that you now know, if you didn't before, that the police are deceitful and have a bag of tricks they use against you, that even if you are innocent, talking to the police can end up with you being convicted of a crime you didn't commit. The legal system is quite the quagmire, and knowing your rights is imperative. The unfortunate fact is that just knowing your rights normally isn't enough. You also need a rainy-day fund stuck away at all times in case you need to hire legal counsel.

If you visit the Supreme Court of the United States of America, you will see a statue. It is of a woman who is blindfolded and holding a scale that is equally balanced. This is to communicate the sentiment that justice is blind, fair, and balanced. I hate to be the one to say it, but nothing could be farther from the truth. The future of this country, as well as the present day, when it comes to law enforcement, and, in all honesty, many other aspects of government, fills me with fear of the world into which our children and grandchildren will step. Something has to be done, and it's going to take a concerted effort of many. This guide is a portion of my little part. God bless you all.

Appendix

1. Don't talk to the police - https://www.youtube.com/watch?v=d-7o9xYp7eE&t=66s

2. Eddie Joe Lloyd. - https://innocenceproject.org/cases/eddie-joe-lloyd/

3. Search and seizure - https://www.youtube.com/watch?v=_4O1OlGyTuU

4. https://www.flexyourrights.org/faqs/top-4-traffic-ticket-myths/

5. https://www.flexyourrights.org/faqs/when-can-police-use-drug-dogs/

6. Police Integrity Lost: A Study of Law Enforcement Officers Arrested - https://www.ojp.gov/pdffiles1/nij/grants/249850.pdf

7. https://www.motor1.com/features/432577/police-request-exit-vehicle-break-law/

8. https://en.wikipedia.org/wiki/Kentucky_v._King#:~:text=The%20Court%20has%20identified%20three,under%20imminent%20threat%20of%20injury

9. http://www.nolocontendere.org/historyofnolo.html

10. Brennancenter.org

11. https://www.law.cornell.edu/supremecourt/text/367/643

12. https://www.pewresearch.org/fact-tank/2019/06/11/only-2-of-federal-criminal-defendants-go-to-trial-and-most-who-do-are-found-guilty/

13. https://www.youtube.com/watch?v=8ne6uRvQg2U

Back Cover

Thomas B. Fitzgerald, aka TFitz, is a software engineer who has found himself involved in his fair share of police interactions: good and bad. This guide is the culmination of those events. TFitz offers a no holds barred view in regards to any sort of interaction with law enforcement, and offers practical advice to help you when the time comes. At 20 years old, his residence was surrounded by jump-out boys, claiming probable cause for a search after illegally entering the home's curtilage and smelling marijuana.

He was told later, an informant claimed dope was being cooked there. They left with nothing but a few people in handcuffs and a small amount of marijuana. At 23 he was pulled over for improper lane usage. Sober, yet refused to blow. Much money and time later, he was found not guilty of any charges. That night the arresting officer had broken the record for number of DUI arrests.

Currently he is doing all he can to fight for the most important person in his life, his son. He is an outstanding father & role model, and there is nothing in the world he wouldn't do to protect Zeke (his son). He has been awaiting trial for 1.5 years on false accusations of domestic violence. During that time he has met many others who have family members currently jailed over lies and others' abuses of our legal system. He is doing his part to help change that with the organization Women Against False Accusations. If you are interested, search TFitz on YouTube; he'll be there. Please send prayers and love to all.

Made in the USA
Monee, IL
04 November 2026

67387886R00046